Praise for Li

'Poignant, witty, straig
Joanna L

'Plant a smile c
You Magazine

'The poetry of slugs, lost trowels, herbaceous-border anxiety and downing tools for the holidays!'
BBC Radio 4 Saturday Live

'Funny, bittersweet.'
Mail on Sunday

'Light-hearted.'
Scottish Herald

'Will chime with every gardener.'
English Garden

'Perfect for the busy reader and mum.'
Sainsbury Magazine

'Gardening gems.'
Lancashire Evening Post

'Warm, witty, incisive.'
Worcester News

'Our favourite.'
The Lady

'What you need is a dose of Liz Cowley's quick wit.'
Sunday World

'Entertaining.'
Irish Independent

'Laugh.'
Metro, Dublin

'Short, bitter-sweet.'
Metrolife

'A delight for the nation's army of avid gardeners.'
Lancaster Guardian

'The people's poet.'
Blackpool Gazette

'Britain's only gardening poet.'
Beverley Guardian

'Packed with the dogged spirit of gardeners.'
Bridlington Free Press

'Warm and winsome.'
Isle of Man Today

'Gems of outdoor observation.'
The Clitheroe Advertiser and Times

'Making us laugh and lifting our spirits.'
Longridge News

'Perfect... to relax with.'
Spalding Guardian

'Guaranteed to strike a chord with gardeners.'
Pocklington Post

'The joys and frustrations of gardening.'
The Visitor

'A natural poet in the natural world.'
The St Helens Reporter

'Much to smile about.'
Pendle Today

'Funny, piquant poetry.'
Lytham St Annes Express

'Whimsical.'
Leyland Guardian

'This garden of delights.'
Leigh Reporter

'The ideal gift for gardeners good... and bad!'
Garstang Courier

'Nothing escapes her notice.'
Fleetwood Weekly News

'Enjoy.'
Driffield Times & Post

'Familiar gardening dilemmas.'
Chorley Guardian

'Poetic gems.'
Bridlington Free Press

'Wickedly funny.'
Burnley Express

GREEN FINGERS

LIZ COWLEY

GIBSON SQUARE

This edition published for the first time by Gibson Square

UK Tel: +44 (0)20 7096 1100
US Tel: +1 646 216 9813

rights@gibsonsquare.com
www.gibsonsquare.com

ISBN 9781783341504

Papers used by Gibson Square are natural, recyclable products made from wood grown in sustainable forests; inks used are vegetable based. Manufacturing conforms to ISO 14001, and is accredited to FSC and PEFC chain of custody schemes. Colour-printing is through a certified CarbonNeutral® company that offsets its CO2 emissions.

Printed by Clays.

I

I

'The earth is like a child that knows poems by heart.'
Rainer Maria Rilke

Spring

Green fingers

Oh, much much greener fingers
some gardening friends have got.
I don't much like my fingers,
for green they're often not.
I've seen much greener fingers
in someone else's place.
My fingers cannot match theirs,
but green can be my face!

Up in the morning's no for me,
Up in the morning early.

Robert Burns (1759-96), Scottish poet and lyricist

Up in the morning – not for you?
Up in the morning early?
You missed the nicest time of day –
before the hurly-burly!

Up in the morning *is* for me –
up in the morning early,
when half the world is still asleep
(or is awake, but surly).

Up in the morning is for me.
By five o'clock I'm waking,
and then, wide-eyed, I'm soon outside
when each new day is breaking.

Up in the morning is for me,
you'll find me out there roaming –
and still clad in my dressing gown
with hair in need of combing.

Up in the morning is for me,
perhaps to do some weeding,
and greet my robin every day
who always needs some feeding.

Up in the morning is for me
to see what's out there growing –
in common with most gardeners:
first place where we'll be going.

You're up and out there early too?
We understand each other –
we're part of a great sisterhood.
Or maybe you're a brother!

When you enter the garden,
you are the rose of roses,
and also the lily of lilies.

J.W. von Goethe (1749-1832)

That's something never ever said to me –
and in the morning, not surprisingly!
'The rose of roses?' No one would agree.
Thank God there's no one out there who can see.
'Lily of lilies'? Oh, good heavens, no!
Thank goodness I'm alone, and not on show.
It's lucky no one's out there to condemn
if I look like a wreck at six a.m..
But later on, it would be heaven-sent
if someone gave me such a compliment!

Everyone is more or less mad at one point.

'Plain Tales from the Hills' by Rudyard Kipling (1865-1936)

What *am* I doing planting –
and in the pouring rain?
Do other gardeners do that?
Are they, like me, insane?

What am I doing out here?
The plants can wait – and me.
So why the rush to do things –
and do them instantly?

Everyone is mad on one point,
or more or less – and gardeners more.
In fact, the gardeners that I know
are often mad on three or four.

Of all the things I have each year
(some sparkling bright and glowing).
I think the things I hold most dear
are the ones so bright and growing.

Of all the gifts I have each year
I also love things growing,
but sparkly things like pretty rings –
they make a rarer showing!

Of all the things I have each year,
most presents are for planting,
but oh, alas, I can't recall
a jewel quite enchanting!

Of all the things I have each year
(none sparkling bright and glowing)
I think the one *I'd* hold most dear
is *not* one that's for growing.

Here's hoping my old man reads this.
It might just get him going.
A sparkly thing – perhaps a ring –
has been a long time owing!

Forgetfulness is a form of freedom.

Kahlil Gibran (1883-1931)

'Liz, aren't you coming in to do the lunch?'
My husband calls me from the kitchen door.
Help! I'd quite forgotten asking friends round.
And who? I can't remember any more.

Eight for lunch; no time to do the shopping.
Now what to do? They're here in half an hour.
Order several pizzas? I'd feel guilty.
Not even time to have a decent shower.

What's the time? Good God, I can't believe it!
I must have been outside since ten to eight.
Tell my friends the lunch has just been cancelled?
Oh God, I can't do that; it's far too late.

Time outside can make me absent-minded,
beguiled, besotted, in a total trance,
quite forgetting people I've invited
while choosing pleasant places for my plants.

Planting out soon puts me in a dream world;
all part, I think, of what a garden's for.
Then the dreaming fast becomes a nightmare
when friends arrive too early at the door.

Ouch! They're here, while I'm still in the bathroom!
There's nothing I can do but go on down.
Where's my husband? Gone to do the shopping.
I'll have to greet them in my dressing gown!

The word allotment now starts with 'W'

My friend Tony Hannaford

'Why? Well, when you think about it,
so much there starts with 'w'.
Allotment doesn't start with 'a'
as long ago it used to do.

Wellies, lots of winsome widows
and widowers upon the plot,
and wearisome – those worriers,
if well-kept, weed-free your spot's not.

And waiting lists, long waiting lists
before you even win a spot,
and when at last allotted one,
it's one you wish you hadn't got.

The W.I.? Oh, they'll be there
to wow you with their wizard fruit.
Lots of warm, well-meaning types
who've joined The Women's Institute.

Others – whistlers, wearisome,
in well-worn clothes as oft as not,
like woolly hats and windcheaters.
Well, no one cares who's wearing what.

And weekend gardeners wanting space
where they can find tranquillity –
a place to wind down out of town,
but pushed to keep their plots weed-free.

Often wild and whacky types
who don't have that much time to weed,
so end with wastelands on the plot
in which a million weevils breed.

That's not counting wet spells, whitefly
soon wiping out what's on their plot,
and, much worse, committee windbags
with all the petty rules they've got.

Weird whisperers who wander round
and love to wield authority,
while waving wretched warning cards
if plots are not kept tidily.

All woeful people watching you
while *you* wait for the next complaint,
especially if you're like me
and often use your plot to paint.

They wail 'It's not a studio!'
and say that it's a waste of space
when other more deserving souls
have waited ages for a place.

And if yours is a wilderness
as mine can very often be,
well, then you won't be welcome there.
In fact, they've just evicted me.'

Wow, would I want allotment space?
Not now it starts with 'w'.
Too much worry, too much warfare.
Who'd want a space like that – do you?

I wouldn't want the rules (and fools)
who tell plot owners what to do,
although I'd love to grow the veg
I don't have space for – that is true.

How nice to eat that healthily.
But all that hassle? Not for me,
especially as veg seems to be
a decent price in Sainsbury.

The true paradises are the paradises we have lost.

Time Regained *by Marcel Proust (1871-1922)*

'Have an apple, darling.'
'No!' Dad said, 'Leave them be!'
'Why? I've had a nibble,
and look – it's not harmed me.
What's the point of apples,
this many on a tree,
if not allowed to eat them?
Well, none that I can see.

Why did Dad make apples
and hang them on a tree
if the fruit's forbidden?
That makes no sense to me.
The serpent thinks he's silly,
and, frankly, I agree.
Eve, love, taste this apple
and picnic here with me!

What's the point of apples
we're not allowed to taste?
If that is heaven's logic,
I think it's such a waste.
Evict us both for eating
an apple on a tree?
No loving dad would do that.
That's crazy, please trust me.

Oh Lord, I see him coming,
and looking cross with me!
But why? For just one apple?
Loads more upon the tree.
And who would want this Eden,
and garden all alone
with no one else to notice
the lovely plants you've grown?

A lonely place, this Eden,
without our company.
And who'd do all the gardening?
It's hard enough with three.
The old man couldn't manage,
up here and on his own.
Without us, all of Eden
would soon be overgrown.'

'My God, he's sounding angry!
He's in a frightful state.
Gosh, Adam, what's he shouting?'
'He wants us through the gate.'
'What for? One silly apple?
He won't get rid of us.
Evict us, for an apple?
That's quite ridiculous!'

Is there no way out of the mind?

Sylvia Plath (1932-63)

Yes, Sylvia, there *is* a way
if what's in there is bleak or sad
or deeply troubled and disturbed
and thoughts you have are mostly bad.
Yes, for all that, there's a way out.
I couldn't recommend it more.
But where? Which way? Not far away.
Try walking through your garden door.
If your mind is plunged in turmoil,
it's well worth giving it a chance.
Nothing in this life's more calming
than contemplating flowers and plants.

As soon as one is unhappy, one becomes moral.

Marcel Proust (1871-1922)

Gardeners, I think, are mostly happy.
Does that make us less moral? Surely not.
And many of us dwell while gardening
on all our blessings others haven't got.

Gardeners, of course, aren't always happy,
but gardens calm us at the times we're not –
telling us that we are truly lucky,
and more so when the world has lost the plot.

Gardeners are also quite reflective,
and dwelling on our own contentedness
possibly think even more of others
who struggle through their lives with so much less.

Misery, morality – twin sisters?
Less moral if we're happy? Surely, no.
Outside gardening, counting all our blessings,
our sympathy for others may well grow.

When you're bored with yourself, marry and be bored with someone else.

David Pryce-Jones (1936-)

My God, what a depressing thought!
Far better, take up gardening.
Get married? Bored with someone else?
How could you think of such a thing?

Not kind to the other person
to load your boredom on to them,
not good for the marriage either –
soon headed for a requiem!

All people bored – and by themselves –
should look outside – and literally.
A hobby may be waiting there
that changes life – and instantly.

But what if gardening's not your bag,
and then you find that boring too?
Well then, you seem a hopeless drag.
I'm sorry, I give up on you!

Gardening requires lots of water – most of it in the form of perspiration.

Louise Erickson (1928-)

And, for me, a glass of rosé
to celebrate the planting's done,
and a round of Pimm's in summer
enjoyed outside beneath the sun;
and perhaps stiff gin in winter
when all is looking bleak and grey,
or at times I've put my back out
while clearing all the sludge away.
All as well as lots of water –
and mostly perspiration, true.
But endless sweat? A better bet
is loads of relaxation too.
I find your comment full of fun,
you sound a witty soul, that's true.
But give yourself a rest, Louise.
Sit back sometimes – enjoy the view!

Friendship needs a certain parallelism of life, a community of thought, a rivalry of aim.

The Education of Henry Adams *by Henry Brooks Adams (1838-1918)*

A certain parallelism – yes.
But why a rivalry of aim?
Most gardeners will make splendid friends,
although our thinking's not the same.
Quite different many aims may be,
but does that lead to argument?
Not at all. We simply differ,
and doing so, we're quite content.

Friendship needs some parallels
and some community of thought,
but if we have our differences
it doesn't cut the friendship short.
In fact, friends may well add to it
and make our lives more interesting,
and rivals we need never be
with different views on gardening.

The seeds of doubt

Useful test with largish seeds:
just pour cold water in a pan,
and those that float you shouldn't plant,
and those that quickly sink, you can.

Always remember the beauty of the garden, for there is peace

There's no peace if we're near Heathrow.
The planes start coming in at five.
We have to get up after that,
and often feeling half-alive.

And then the planes fly all day long.
Two minutes, there's another one.
Peace? There's not much in the garden,
Those endless planes are not much fun.

But, strangely, we get used to it
and suddenly don't hear the roar.
And then, at last, we feel the peace
we never could enjoy before.

Soon we're deaf to interruptions
like people knocking at the door,
as well as noisy aeroplanes
we're not aware of any more.

All gardeners always use their eyes.
But deaf we gardeners can be
when blocking out the daily din
that interrupts tranquillity.

But I'm not so think as you drunk I am.

'Ballade of Soporific Absorption' by Sir John Collings Squire (1884-1958)

They told you *that* when on their way?
There's nothing much that you can say!
That's if they stay for lunch all day
and steal your planting hours away.

The world is a much worse place than I ever thought it.

W.R. Inge, (1860-1954)

A Dean to say that? Curious.
No gardener then, it's obvious.
If everything seemed quite so grim,
a garden could have lifted him.
I have to say I find it odd –
those words, and from a man of God.
When so depressed by mortal sin,
a garden – best place to be in.
The world then seems a kinder place
and one that's easier to face –
much better than it was before
since stepping through your garden door.

It is better to die on your feet than live on your knees.

'La Pasionara', Dolores Ibárruri (1895-1983)

Today I have no choice in that –
impossible with two duff knees.
A kneeler? You can count me out.
A present that I don't want, please!

I think I'll die when standing up
and bending over some nice plant,
then crashing in a flowerbed
as getting to my knees, I can't!

The most precious things in speech are pauses.

Ralph Richardson (1902-83)

Most precious things in gardens too –
the pauses, times in which to think,
the silences to dwell on life –
especially when our spirits sink.

Pauses – needed more than ever –
the time to be with plants and flowers
and have a bit of hush, not rush,
so hectic is this world of ours.

Traffic jams, computer glitches,
and deadlines, family rifts – the lot,
building problems, breakdowns, meltdowns –
no wonder we can lose the plot.

A garden – a great antidote,
that acts at times like soothing balm –
and then restores one's brain again
and helps us rediscover calm.

And makes us wonder why we're here,
and think about the world a bit,
and offers us a sanctuary
from all the hell we see in it.

Either the wallpaper goes, or I do.

Oscar Wilde (1854-1900), looking at the wallpaper around his deathbed

Floral paper, not for Oscar,
and floral paper, not for me.
Dear Oscar, what a way to go.
I have the greatest sympathy.

Lest we forget.

'Recessional' by Rudyard Kipling (1865-1936)

'Forget me not'? Why would we?
I've often wondered why.
Why would we all forget you?
And who would walk on by?

'Forget me not'. How could we,
with that great shade of blue?
How *could* we walk on past you
with such a gorgeous hue?

But still, the name so suits you,
although it's a surprise.
How could we all forget you,
as blue as summer skies?

A flower picked by lovers
who said 'Forget me not'?
Perhaps that's how the name came:
that could explain a lot.

The grass is always greener on the other side of the fence

I wish! Today there's horrid asphalt
or concrete where they park the car.
I wish that grass *was* there, and greener.
So dull today, front gardens are.

I don't know whether I believe in God or not.

Henri Matisse (1869-1954)

You sound the same as me, Henri.
I think about it quite a lot,
and *can* believe when gardening,
but then, back in the house, cannot.

God, for me, lives only outside.
I stop believing coming in,
except when I have brought in flowers.
Belief then wears a bit less thin.

God's face I *can* see in a plant
as every one's a miracle –
a thing no human could create
or ever make as beautiful.

God's face I can't see in the house,
or nowhere near as easily,
except when watching gardeners
on garden programmes on TV.

Does that make me an oddity?
Oh no, I've never thought it rare
to lose one's faith in God inside,
but sometimes, outside, find it there.

You're probably a bit like me –
besieged by disbelief and doubt
but aometimes, with refreshed belief
when plants and flowers are coming out.

United we stand, divided we fall.

Aesop (Sixth century BC)

Not exactly a plant anthem.
United weak, divided strong.
Often, if not separated,
many plants won't live that long.
Many types that start united
will scream to be divided fast.
Not relocated instantly
(as many should be) they won't last.
Plants can be so unlike people,
lots yearning to be on their own,
in need of space and their own place,
and relishing their lives alone.

Blessed are the horny hands of toil.

'A glance behind the curtain' by James Russell Lowell (1819-91)

Not many gardeners would agree with that,
as gardeners (proper gardeners) don't wear gloves.
We cannot feel the plant and what it's doing,
and end with hands that nobody much loves.
Gardening hands are older than our faces
and rarely any source of vanity.
Blessèd are the horny hands of gardeners?
The hand that's writing this would disagree!

The more, the merrier

Well said! I'm more than with you there.
I've never much liked minimal,
or gardens that I see in shows,
so often stark and sculptural.

I love a border crammed with plants,
the more the merrier for me.
I'm firmly an old-fashioned type,
and also quite content to be.

The trend – a 'garden architect'
who pares things down, with far less plants,
and puts in far more man-made things.
Would I employ one? Not a chance!

'The more, the merrier' – old hat.
Today the norm is 'less is more'
but not what I would want to see
when going through my garden door.

I don't want things like mirrors there;
on all that sort of thing I'll pass.
I simply want plants everywhere,
and in between them, lots of grass.

The funky stuff can stay in shows
and minimal is not for me,
especially when it comes to plants.
I like a lot of company!

It is not swinish to be happy unless one is happy in swinish ways.

Susan Stebbing (1885-1943)

No, not swinish to be happy,
unless one is in swinish ways,
or 'wine-ish' ways you should have said
when eating out on balmy days.

Or *drinking* out – more accurate,
and starting on the plonk at noon –
and then, our downfall (literally),
continuing all afternoon.

No, not swinish to be happy,
or even to be overfed,
but 'wine-ish' – that's embarrassing
when toppling in a flowerbed!

That's happened here, and more than once,
people toppling on to flowers.
It's best to let them sleep it off,
though that can take them several hours!

They wake – and everyone's gone home –
a moment so embarrassing,
especially if plants were squashed
beneath them when recovering.

How to phone and say a thank you?
They don't a while, and keep away.
Please don't expect them calling up
before they've worked out what to say.

They need to think before they call,
but know that won't be any use.
At times there's nothing friends can say,
or nothing that's a good excuse!

That sprinkler is at it again
hissing and spitting its arc
of silver, and the parched
lawn is tickled green.

from 'The Summer Day' by Ruth Pitter (1897-1992), British poet

My sprinkler is at it again,
dribbling to nothing, but why?
Or suddenly stopping, which leaves me quite hopping,
or drenching me as I walk by.

My sprinkler is at it again.
Why is the damned thing so mean?
Mine doesn't 'tickle', it goes to a trickle –
no wonder the grass isn't green.

But *what* makes it suddenly stop?
Perhaps it's a kink in the hose,
though I've checked it to see why it's so mean to me,
and dozens of times, goodness knows.

My sprinkler – a mind of its own.
It teases me, time and again,
and chucks off the hose, so little grass grows.
I think I'll just wait for the rain.

All poets are mad.

The Anatomy of Melancholy by Robert Burton (1577-1640)

I think you're right – all gardeners too.
All have a streak of madness – true.
And what on earth is one to do
if born a mixture of the two?
Pruners, choppers, re-arrangers,
all poets, gardeners – similar –
and never quite content with things –
I think all parties would concur.
All poets mad, all gardeners too,
compelled to change things all the time,
whether it's with growing flowers
or always re-arranging rhyme.

What is a weed? A plant whose virtues have never been discovered.

Ralph Waldo Emerson (1803-82)

Ralph, lots of plants we label 'weeds'
have virtues that are long well known,
and many years before your time
as history has clearly shown.

Cuisine and homeopathy
and medicine – weeds are part of that.
For someone born in 1803
your words, already, were old hat.

A thousand weeds have well-known virtues
though not, quite clearly, known to you.
I rather like your witty thought,
although it plainly isn't true.

Did you not cook a sorrel soup
or taste the leaves of dandelion,
or ever sip a nettle soup?
(You should have done; great source of iron!)

What, never make a daisy chain,
or else a wine from elderflower,
or sip tea made of chamomile
and feel its soothing, healing power?

Weeds – plants whose virtues *were* discovered,
and well before your time, old chap.
It seems you never stopped to think
before you wrote those words. What crap!

Blessed are my well-worn and much loved gardening tools that have never let me down.

'Beatitudes for the Gardener' by Gail Kavanagh

Your tools have never let you down?
Where *do* you buy your tools? I ask.
Mine snap or break or hide from me.
Replacement is a common task.

You must be great at maintenance
and also spend as many hours
on looking after all of them
as tending to your plants and flowers.

A lot of tools have let me down.
What's more, it always seems to me,
they do so on the very day
it's just run out, the guarantee.

To be an adult is to be alone.

Pensées *by Jean Rostand (1894-1977)*

Sad thing to say – a shame you felt that way.
But true? I find I can't agree with you.
I don't see all adults as lone islands,
as you so clearly (and so bleakly) do.

And, to be alone has many good points –
the time to work things out in our own space.
But *feel* alone – now that is very different,
as if divided from the human race.

Not to be alone, for many gardeners,
would often interrupt our hopes and dreams.
Alone, we're often at our happiest.
Not true for you, it very clearly seems.

What a sad, bleak comment, Monsieur Rostand,
'To be an adult is to be alone.'
Being adults doesn't mean we're loners.
It only means that we are fully grown.

Thou shalt love thy neighbour as thyself

Leviticus 19:18

Not if your neighbour poisons your creeper,
not if your neighbour complains of your trees.
Not if your neighbour moans about parties,
not if your neighbour is so hard to please.
Not if your neighbour grumps about children,
not if your neighbour can't give you a smile.
Not if your neighbour can't say 'Good morning!'
You'd want her gone, and at least by a mile!

Not if your neighbour loves macracarpa,
and not if your neighbour blocks out your light.
Not if your neighbour leaves out the rubbish
for foxes to scatter – a horrible sight.
Not if your neighbour says your horse chestnut
is growing too tall and toppling her wall.
Not if your neighbour's always complaining.
Love her? Forget it. You wouldn't at all!

The foolish man seeks happiness in the distance; the wise grows it under his feet.

James Oppenheim (1882-1932)

A thought I love, so flattering to gardeners,
and one that seems so strongly-felt and wise.
But if we travel, then we see our gardens
much refreshed, and with quite different eyes.
Returning, we like gardens all the better
and know exactly where we're most at home.
But travelling also broadens our horizons.
It's good at times, inspiring too, to roam.

Seeking happiness in distant places
is not because we don't like what's behind.
Maybe, Oppenheim, you should have said that,
and possibly have been a bit more kind.
What is wrong with happiness in gardens,
and happiness in distant places too?
Both can surely complement the other.
I travel, and I know that can be true.

Look before you leap

I know I always should when buying plants,
unless of course, I know just what they are.
and also take a magnifying glass,
so teeny weeny all advice tips are.

Loads of languages on every label,
so English tips are in a tiny size.
Hard to read, when even wearing glasses,
especially for those with older eyes.

Enthusiastic people are most gardeners,
but also pretty scatty many are.
Lots of us rush off to garden centres,
and then, like me, leave glasses in the car.

'WEAR THEM ROUND YOUR NECK!' my husband bellows.
The one and only time that he's unkind.
'What's the point of coming to a centre
and rushing into things when you're half-blind?'

Go back to the car and get my glasses?
I can't. The car park's much too far away.
Take the plants back? Unpack the whole trolley?
I don't. I simply say that *I* will pay.

If I've made mistakes, I'll say it's my fault.
'I promise you, you won't hear me complain.'
'Fine. But Liz, *do* wear your bloody glasses,
or *don't* expect me in this place again!'

Come rain, come shine

Come rain, come shine, you'll find us out
(unless it's truly pelting down –

then, of course, it's quite depressing
when watching favourite flowers drown).
But if it's just sporadic rain
or else a spate of April showers,
then we'll still be out there gardening –
and pottering for hours and hours.

The fruit never falls far from the tree

It's clear you've never owned a sycamore.
Its fruits spread everywhere; great distances.
I know, because I have a sycamore
and know, each Autumn, what a bore it is.

All winged fruits can fly. You've never noticed?
That shouldn't come as any big surprise.
And what's the point of having wings at all,
if fruit that they're attached to never flies?

Start as you mean to go on

That would make for dreary gardening!
What? Never try out something new?
And never look at modern trends,
or think how you might change the view?
Much better to experiment
and not go on the same old way,
though keeping favourite plants, of course –
the ones you'd hate to throw away.
Why just plough on as you started,
without a change of scenery

or else a different colour scheme?
How very boring that would be!
A change is good for all of us –
as good, it's said, as is a feast.
And gardens that stay just the same
are ones I tend to like the least.

A man travels the world in search of what he needs and returns home to find it.

George Moore (1852-1933)

Never more than gardeners.
We see the world, we like to roam,
and then returning to our gardens,
we know just where we're most at home.
First thing we do when getting back?
Unpacking cases? Very rare.
We're quickly at the garden door
to see what's changed since last time there.

And checking emails? Big, *big* no.
We're out there looking at our plants,
and as for opening paper mail,
with gardeners there is little chance.
And phone our friends to say we're back?
No, not until we've been outside,
concerned that in a fortnight off
some much-loved plants could well have died.

Spotting if the daily's been there?
Oh no, we're not that fussed by dust!
But go outside, we gardeners will –
without delay, we know we must.
Cases dumped within the hallway,
we're out there, seeing what to do,

and though we love to see the world
we're glad the holiday is through.

We search the world for what we need
and then we find it back at home.
A private place, a soothing space
in which we're free to think and roam.
We search the world for what we need
and find it through the garden door:
a hush amidst the constant rush,
the best thing to be searching for.

God moves in a mysterious way.

William Cowper (1731-1800)

Our globe may simply be one tiny cell
that's buried deep within the brain of God,
a God too vast to even contemplate,
though human brains may find that concept odd.

The universe and everything we see
may be no bigger than a single pea;
one cell within a giant deity –
too large to contemplate by you and me.

What if this world, the universe we're in
were even smaller than a drawing pin,
just one of many cells within God's skin –
and understanding that we can't begin?

Our brains are limited by what we see,
and possibly by God, intentionally.
It's hard to think that what our globe could be
is just one dot within a deity.

I think most gardeners muse on things like that.
It sometimes goes with gardening, I find.
It worries me, at times, that all we see
is just a speck that's buried in God's mind.

There's a sucker born every minute

Words for every owner of Catalpa –
a lifetime pruning lies ahead of you.
Every minute there's another sucker
that grows enormous in a week or two.

Quite gorgeous it may be, this lovely tree,
but all those suckers drive one bloody mad.
But chop mine down? I can't. It's beautiful,
unlike the endless pruning days I've had.

Gardeners are among the most relaxed people (when they're gardening) that you'll find.

The Little Book of Calm *by Paul Wilson*

And when *not* gardening, is that also true?
I'd tend to say so, and maybe you do.
Temper is rarer in gardeners, I find,
perhaps because gardens help us unwind.
Or it's because we can stomp off outside,
and before taking anyone's side,
and sit there in silence and slug a stiff gin
when patience is wearing thoroughly thin.
Rows are much harder to have 'en plein air'.
What's more, the neighbours may well hear us there!

The higher above the ground you feel, the closer you will be to feeling calm.

The Little Book of Calm *by Paul Wilson*

The closer to the ground I am,
the more I'm likely to feel calm –
I guess like every gardener.
That's part of every garden's charm.

The more removed from earth we are,
the less relaxed and calm we'll be.
Indeed, it's earth that earths us most,
and helps us live contentedly.

We're stressed, we're strained, fed up with life,
but then, once through the garden door,
a calm descends, and all at once
some things don't matter any more.

It is no coincidence that serious meditators, yogis, ascetics, martial artists and many religious orders treat the moments before sunrise as the most precious of the day.

The Little Book of Calm *by Paul Wilson*

Paul, you left us gardeners out.
Why? Few of us are sleepyheads;
up and out and wandering
as soon as we have left our beds.

Up and out before the sunrise,
exactly like the folk you quote.
Next time you write a book of calm,
that's something you may wish to note.

(Or perhaps you *did* include us,
as meditators gardeners are;
dreamers in the early morning,
no sooner through the garden door.

Not like yogis or ascetics,
but meditators certainly,
drinking in those precious moments
that help to save our sanity).

If seven maids with seven mops swept it for half a year, do you suppose, the walrus said, that they could get it clear?

Through the Looking Glass *by Lewis Carroll (1832-98)*

No, not with oak trees high above,
like on my patio.
It's never leafless, all year round.
Each day, loads more below.
If seven maids with seven mops
mopped up for half a year,
they'd waste their time. A hundred sacks
would soon be needed here.
The first six months, that's bad enough,
the last six – even worse.
And seven maids with seven mops
would never end the curse.
Do *you* have oak trees in your place,
and near the house, like me,
and spend your winters budging sludge?
Too kind to them are we.
It's hard to chop down ancient trees
despite the leaves they shed,
although I often picture it –
a flowerbed instead!

I think that I shall never see a poem lovely as a tree.

Joyce Kilmer (1886-1918)

I think that I will often see
a poem lovely as a tree,
but what I know with certainty –
it won't be one that's done by me!

Grow what you love, the love will keep it growing

Alas, that isn't always true,
since much depends upon your plot.
And which way does your garden face?
Well, that will matter quite a lot.
All the love you pour on plants
is wasted if their home's not right,
and plants are temperamental too,
when even in the perfect site.
For instance, I love lavender,
but sadly it won't grow for me.
It couldn't be much clearer proof
you wrote those words mistakenly.
It faces south, I water it,
but still it shrivels every year.
And finally I've given up
and know that I can't grow it here.
Your words are charming, that is true,
but sadly, also fanciful.
Love isn't always given back.
Some plants are not that dutiful.

A blessing in my mouth, those pale hard pods which I taste even now as I chew on this memory.

'Shelling peas' by Penny Harter(1940-)

I sat there shelling peas like you did as a tot.
A blessing in my mouth? Good heavens, firmly not!

In those days shelling peas was never any fun,
as maggots lived in pods, and almost every one.

What? Shelling peas a wheeze? I find that rather odd,
as most peas had disease, and God, who'd eat the pod?

'A blessing in your mouth?' Well, Penny, not for me.
No, not with squirming babes surrounding every pea.

But then, you're getting on, some years ahead of me,
and maybe things have gone, like chunks of memory?

'A blessing' in your mouth?' Peas, not like that for me!
Or maybe those you shelled were far less maggoty?

Delay the time you do things and then the moment's gone

Outside again in slippers –
now covered with wet mud.
I've gone to see the cherry
that's coming into bud.
Boots beside the back door –
a bore to pull them on.
Delay the time you do things
and then the moment's gone.

I need a stash of slippers –
and washable, each pair.
But only black and brown ones;
there's often mud out there.

If gardens draw you outside,
and often at first light,
then pretty feathered slippers w
will soon be black as night.
And ones with heels? Disaster!
They'd soon sink in the mud.
But drag on wellies daily?
That's not in gardeners' blood.

Delay the time you do things,
and then the moment's gone.
What gardeners would be bothered
to pull their wellies on?

I am I plus my surroundings, and if I do not preserve the latter, I do not preserve myself.

'Meditationes del Quijote' by José Ortega y Gasset (1883-1955)

José must have been a gardener.
His words describe us perfectly.
Not preserving our surroundings
we'd all live pretty miserably.

Not preserving what is out there
and letting it become a mess
is hardly a great recipe
for inner calm, contentedness.

You are you, plus your surroundings,
and so am I, and so am I –
like every other gardener –
so intertwined we are, that's why.

If we don't preserve our gardens
I think we tend to lose the plot,
and miserable we then become –
a lot when gardens go to pot!

A time to be born and a time to die

Ecclesiastes 3.2

The scribe who wrote that surely studied nature
and spent a great deal of his life outside.
Few things earth us more than plants within it,
and watching them from birth until they've died.

In those words, I see a calm acceptance,
a tranquil way to live and then to die.
Is that why a lot of us are gardeners?
Well, maybe it's another reason why.

Two mothers is too much

Having had a mother and a nanny
(and often feeling torn between the two)
Mother's Day was always such a nightmare -
I never ever knew quite what to do.

Flowers for both? Would that upset my mother?
Give Nan a card, and give my mother flowers?
Give two bunches, one a wee bit smaller?
Every year, deciding took me hours.

When you're cherished by a loving nanny,
then Mother's Day can be a misery.
What to do was always agonising
when coping with divided loyalty.

Remind myself that nannies are not mothers
(though mine did rather more to mother me)?
Tell her that I love her like a mother,
but cannot give to her – and equally?

Part-relinquishing the role of mother
or giving someone else the starring role
can make each Mother's Day a total horror,
and make a child a lost and tortured soul.

My solution? Make them both a posy
and take one early to my Nan in bed,
so Mother wouldn't know and wouldn't see it,
and love her posy left downstairs instead.

Patience is a virtue

Hurry up, parsley. Please germinate.
Such a slow grower; too long to wait.
Hurry up, parsley, hurry up, seed.
Slow germinator, last thing I need.
Bored of you, parsley, checking your tray.
No bloody difference day after day.
Patience – a virtue you need with this plant.
Slow to get growing, and hurry, it can't.
Why do I bother to sow out a tray?
No sign of growing for day after day.
Thanks a bunch, parsley, for giving me none.
Such a slow grower – you're never much fun.

It is always the best policy to speak the truth – unless, of course, you are an exceptionally good liar.

Jerome K. Jerome (1859-1927)

A notice in a London railway station:

FOR EVERY TREE THAT WE TAKE DOWN
THAT'S TOO CLOSE TO THE RAILWAY TRACK,
WE PLAN TO PLANT AT LEAST THREE MORE:
BUT SENSIBLY, AND FARTHER BACK.

The lie is in that one word 'plan'.
The planners can plan all they like
and never do a bloody thing –
the sort of claim I so dislike.

And will we ever see three trees
for every one they take away?
I doubt it, as I'm sure you do.
We'll never ever see the day.

Well, who will ever count new trees,
or know what has been taken out?
And sitting in a high-speed train,
how *can* we count new trees about?

Count saplings planted farther back?
My God, we'd need fantastic eyes.
Oh, how I hate false claims like that;
so easy to get out of. *Lies*!

But maybe I am far too harsh.
Perhaps they *will* plant trees in threes,
though tiny ones, of such a size
they're ones that no-one ever sees!

In nature, there are no rewards or consequences, there are punishments.

The Face of Clay *by Horace Annesley Vachell(1861-1955)*

In Nature, there are surely great rewards,
and just as surely, consequences too.
All gardens reap a string of benefits
from those who care for them, as millions do.
All punishments? That's surely most untrue.
It seems to me you didn't use your eyes,
and didn't garden, or go into one.
You didn't? That would come as no surprise.
Just think of fertiliser, Horace dear,
and think of things like weeding, watering.
It seems you never noticed anything
about what people do when gardening.

None would understand your observation.
No garden lover would agree with you.
Rarely have I read a famed quotation
that gets it wrong, as your pen seemed to do.
Punishments abound – we'd all agree there –
but rarely through a gardener's loving hand.
Many quotes I've read on Mother Nature,
but yours – the hardest one to understand.
In Nature, no rewards or consequences?
No, even in the wild, she's far more kind.
Just a simple stroll around a garden
would, oh so easily, have changed your mind.

Go to sleep? I'm afraid I've lost the knack.

Dorothy Parker (1893-1967)

Simple, Dotty, spend a whole day gardening.
Get up at dawn and do not stop 'til eight.
All at once you'll find that you are yawning,
and find you simply cannot stay up late.

Simple, Dotty, spend a whole day digging,
and end it with an hour or so to mow.
Then sit down and have a bit of supper.
You'll soon nod off as busy gardeners know.

Simple, Dotty, lug in fertilizer
until you're knackered by the heavy weight.
One thing I can tell you and can promise –
you won't be in a mood to stay up late!

Loneliness can be conquered only by those who crave solitude.

The Eternal Now' by Paul Tillich (1886-1965)

All gardeners crave a bit of solitude,
and may thus suffer less from loneliness.
In fact, I think we relish time alone.
With plants as friends, it couldn't matter less.

Of course we like some human company;
there's nothing to compare with our close mates.
But loneliness can stop within its tracks
when simply walking through our garden gates.

Plants are there to calm us (or to talk to)
and tell us that our time's not spent in vain.
The solitude to conquer loneliness –
it's there each time that we go out again.

Thanks for the memory.

Leo Robin (1900-1984)

Quite often, walking down a street,
I think how much I'd like to meet
the residents who take such pride
in pleasing passers-by outside.
The gardeners, all so generous,
who garden for the rest of us.
Front gardens often make me pause
and make me want to knock on doors
and thank the gardener who's there
for tempting me to stop and stare.

How pleasant passing houses is
when front plots leave nice memories
and give us inspiration too
for plants to try, new things to do.
Although annoying not to know
the names of several plants you grow.
I ought to take a phone with me
and photograph the ones I see.
But then I'm wary that might be
intruding on your privacy.

In every real man a child is hidden that wants to play.

Friedrich Nietzsche (1844-1900)

Which of us has never chucked a 'cleaver' –
the plant that sticks to anything we wear?
Sticky bristles soon engage with clothing.
What's more, they'll quickly stick to human hair.
Adult men (and women), we'll still chuck them,
and laugh to see them sticking everywhere,
while chuckling that it's also known as 'sweetheart'
although its clingy habits drive us spare.
Every adult should stay fun and playful,
and cleavers prove that many think that's true,
'throwing caution to the winds' – and cleavers –
exactly as we always used to do.

A no show

I'm no big fan of Chelsea.
Too crowded now, the show.
I'd need to be much taller;
around six feet or so.

There's not much point in going
if you can't see the plants.
At my height it's quite hopeless,
there's very little chance.

Crammed behind tall Germans,
or taller still, the Dutch,
I can't say I enjoy it,
or if I do, not much!

Love means never having to say you're sorry.

Love Story *by Erich Segal (1937-2010)*

It doesn't if you leave the bloody hose on
the day before we went on holiday,
and then get home to huge bills from Thames Water
and groan and tell me what we'll have to pay!

But there comes a moment in everybody's life when he must decide whether he'll live among human beings or not – a fool among fools, or a fool alone.

Thornton Wilder (1897-1975)

There is a decent halfway house –
to have a place to go outside,
a fool alone, to see what's grown.
Best compromise I've ever tried.

Out there, you *do* have company,
perhaps not of the human kind,
but company, plants are, for sure,
and always welcoming, I find.

A fool with fools, for half your time.
The other half, a fool alone.
Much better way to live your life,
with half spent with the things you've grown.

Just step outside - escape the fools
(and they might like escaping you).
Accept that there aren't any rules
when are you choosing what to do.

One step forward, two steps back.

Vladimir Ilyich Lenin (1870-1924)

How sad that I have lived to see
the dying days of botany;
now rarely offered, this degree,
at any university.

A botanist – already rare.
We hardly meet them anywhere.
A tragedy, and so unfair
to would-be botanists out there.

To universities, a plea:
bring back degrees in botany,
and graduates who truly see
what threatens our ecology.

You'd say that Latin's far too tough,
(it is for some, not easy stuff).
At school, I found the going rough,
but that excuse is not enough.

Environmental Studies? Fine,
though not to several friends of mine
who see it as the clearest sign
that standards are in sharp decline.

What? No degrees in botany?
What kind of landscape will we see
in one decade, or two or three?
I fear for Britain's scenery.

'Pessimism leads to weakness
and optimism leads to power'.
We believe that at our peril
and every year we'll lose a flower.

II

'All things bright and beautiful,
all creatures great and small'
Cecil Frances Alexander

Summer

I plant the seed, you make it grow.
You send the rain, I work the hoe.

I plant the seed,
birds make it go.
Those bloody thieves!
Why do I sow?

I plant the seed.
Birds notice it.
Leave some behind?
The opposite!

I plant the seed.
And then it goes.
Why bother, then?
God only knows!

I plant the seed.
It disappears.
It's no surprise
I'm left in tears!

Bird-brained

Bird-brained, most birds are not.
As bright as me and you,
especially the tit;
a fabulous IQ.
The blue tit – superstar –
as clever as we are,
and some would even say
they're cleverer by far.
'Bird-brained' – a cruel phrase.
Thick? Not a bit of it!
Our birds deserve more praise,
especially the tit!

That's something to crow about!

A crow is perched up in a tree.
I wonder what it thinks of me?
It's looking down on me again,
and probably with some disdain.
And why? Because I cannot fly
and soar and sweep around the sky?

If I were perching in that tree
and looking at me critically,
I'm sure I'd think of many things –
like life without a pair of wings.
The crow may even pity me,
and maybe all humanity.

I wonder, does it study me
and feel superiority,
or just see a nonentity –
or else, potential enemy?
Just what is going through its brain
when looking down at me again?

While watching me at my front door,
it's thinking something, that's for sure.
But thinking what? I'll never know.
I wish I understood that crow.
Each morning when I'm going out,
there's something more it crows about.

But is it simply warning me
it doesn't like my company?
Not understanding, such a curse –
how creatures judge the universe
and human beings that they see.
So much is still a mystery.

Show pity

An orange speck within my book.
It moves – I take a closer look.
A tiny microscopic dot,
and fearful, scuttling round a lot.
Snap the book shut, end of that.
I'd squash the fragile creature flat.
But don't. I blow it off the page.
I'd like the speck to reach old age.
But what the heck's that tiny speck?
So vulnerable, so mini-sized.
I watch it float into the grass,
while once again, by God surprised.

A butterfly mind

However can a butterfly migrate
and cross whole continents with fragile wings?
Wind and storm-tossed, millions make the journey
escaping all the horrors winter brings.

Biting frosts may kill these fragile creatures,
and so, we know, can falls of winter snow.
Doesn't instinct ever try and tell them
it might be somewhat safer *not* to go?

Miracles they are – our Painted Ladies.
Nine thousand miles – the trip they make each year.
But sadly, of the many millions flying,
not many more than half will reappear.

What propels them all to make the journey?
What makes them trust those, oh so fragile wings?
Why do they migrate? An endless mystery.
To me, one of the very strangest things.

In planes we humans fly to distant countries,
but what if nearly half of us would die?
What tells butterflies that they must risk it?
I very often pause, and wonder why.

Silence is golden

Hush! Hush! A thrush! Don't make a sound!
This shy, shy bird will soon retreat.
It needs a bit of space from us,
and rarely less than thirty feet.

A thrush around? Please, stand your ground!
It's looking for a scrap to eat,
and doesn't welcome us around
or find our company a treat.

Hush! Hush! A thrush! Stay where you are!
This shy, shy bird soon flies away
on hearing just one sound from us,
whatever kindly words we say.

Your tiny footsteps on the grass
(that you can't hear, its ears soon will).
The one way to keep thrushes there
is stay put, absolutely still.

Slowly, silently, now the moon
walks the night in her silver shoon.

'Silver' by Walter de la Mare (1873-1956)

Quickly, silently, now the fox
walks the night in his coat of fur
to raid our neighbour's rubbish sacks –
left out *again*. What's wrong with her?
Why can't she put them in a bin
(or if they're full, the council skip?)
My God, the mess our drive is in –
it's time she got a bit of lip!
Quickly, silently garbage flies
around our place – all bloody night.
And getting up is not much fun–
not when I'm in a rubbish site!

Quickly, silently, now the fox
falls fast asleep within his den
and leaves me with the neighbour's trash
that's blown from next door yet again.
Slowly, silently, came the moon –
as did the fox, and pretty soon,
and damn, I'll now be brushing up
the rubbish 'til this afternoon.
Quickly, angrily, I clear up
and pile stuff in the rubbish bin.
The moon – a boon – great for the fox
if bins aren't where the trash is in!

You never cease to amaze me!

Spiders – you never cease to amaze me!
And now I've discovered that you can *fly*.
It's hard to believe it, even conceive it;
the thought of you spiders roaming the sky.

And you can travel on water like ships,
cleverly using your legs just like sails.
And you're great spinners, absolute winners.
Cease to amaze me? Not one of you fails!

Now a researcher – Doctor Hayashi –
has found out how far you spiders can fly.
A good nineteen miles, and that's in *one* day.
Astonishing creatures – no end to why.

Spinning or sailing, flying or ballooning,
all so athletic and far more than Man.
Cease to amaze me? No, you all faze me.
All of you do so much more than we can.

I like the Brits; they do not eat us

Printed on a shopping bag in France, with a picture of happy frogs

'I like the Brits; they do not eat us.'
Seen on a bag of Calvados.
I'm rather glad we don't eat frogs,
though all the French think that's our loss.
I've always rather liked our frogs.
Since childhood I've been fond of them,
and what I like, and even more –
a noisy, croaking pond of them!

Tweet of the day

Radio Four, BBC

So annoying when one can't hear top notes –
another downside of advancing years.
'Can you hear that?' asks my husband daily.
I often can't, it's too high for my ears.

Please, BBC, can we have more birdsong
that's lower down the scale – round middle C?
I'm sure that many other former fans
get irritated daily, just like me.

Less larks perhaps, more birds like eider ducks.
And blackbirds – perfect! Voices nice and low.
High tweets are a turn off every morning.
And do you want me switching off your show?

Let sleeping dogs lie

That reminds me of my granny
who always buried pets outside.
'Let sleeping dogs lie' said each grave
beneath the names of dogs who'd died.
Muffin, Bouncer, Tinka, Panda –
each gravestone marked a much-loved friend,
reminding her of happy days
before each one had met its end.
'Let sleeping dogs lie' – those four words
are etched upon my memory,
reminding me of all the pets
that made her second family.

Patience is not simply the ability to wait – it's how we behave while were waiting.

Joyce Meyer (1943-), American pastor

'Sorry birds – I hate to keep you waiting.
I know your table's bare and topped with snow.
And I know you're absolutely starving.
But come outside? It's far too cold to go!

Yes, I know you're waiting for your breakfast.
I also know the temperature's shot down.
Much too cold to come outside and feed you.
I'd freeze to death out in my dressing gown.

Thank the Lord you're dressed in fluffy feathers
and do not feel the cold within your feet.
Puff those feathers up until I feed you.
Quite soon I'll give you something nice to eat.

Sorry, feathered friends, please show your patience.
I won't come outside now with all that snow.
Keep your feathers ruffled 'til I feed you.
I'll only be a half an hour or so.

Humans do not own a coat of feathers.
We can't stay out too long in ice or snow.
Wait there, birdies; show a bit of patience.
I promise you, there's not too long to go!'

No helpless thing, I cannot harm thee now.
Depart in peace, thy little life is safe.

'The caterpillar' by Anna Letitia Barbauld (1743-1825)

Anna found a caterpillar and let the creature live.
She knew it could destroy her plants, but found she could forgive.
She felt a sense of fellowship, unable then to kill.
One day, with ruined vegetables, I rather think she will.

Anna found a caterpillar, and let the creature go,
And rather kinder Anna was than anyone I know.
Her killer instinct disappeared, the caterpillar too.
I bet she lost her cabbages before the night was through.

We're closer to the ants than to the butterflies.
Very few people can endure much leisure.

'Thoughts in a dry season' by Gerald Brenan (1894-1987)

True, I think of older gardeners.
We always like new tasks to do,
and do not like retirement much
though tasks outside help pull us through.
Much closer to the ants we are,
though some of us are butterflies
and flitting off to distant spots
now freed from all our other ties.
I'm far from any butterfly,
although I like to flit abroad,
but never, I am glad to say,
because at home I'm getting bored.

A glass ceiling

A sparrow's in the house – in our conservatory,
and flying into glass, so terrified is he.

He's whirling all around and getting desperate now,
but how to get him out? I cannot work out how.

He's flying far too high, he will not come on down.
He's doomed with all that glass. I feel my spirits drown.

The poor thing's getting weak. It's sapped his energy.
And now, from way above, he sadly looks at me.

I open wide the doors, and jam a little ledge
between them with some crumbs. I wait...he's at the
edge!

He rests there for a while, and eats a crumb or two,
then chirrups me with thanks – a lovely thing to do.

He flutters, preens his wings. He's off, he flies away!
So terrified was I he'd kill himself today.

Each flower holds a story.

Do Tell *by Martha K. Baker*

And often it's a murder story
when slugs have got into the pot –
one that has no happy ending
as all slugs tend to eat a lot.

Each flower holds a story – true,
but one I may not want to hear –
depending on the bugs and slugs
which may mean plants will disappear.

Every flower holds a story,
and often with a tragic end
when slugs have all but ruined it
and driven gardeners round the bend.

Too many of their stories – short,
with chapters we don't want to read,
far too often bleak, depressing,
because of predators – and greed.

III

'The livin' is easy.'

from Porgy and Bess by Ira Gershwin

Summer is icumen in

'Cuckoo Song', a medieval rota

'Good morning! Welcome to my class.
I always knew you'd reappear.
I'm sure you'll paint a masterpiece –
you should do, at this time of year.

So many flowers coming out,
so many hues that you can choose.
My springtime class had quite a few,
but far, far less than you can use.

And autumn students often moan
they're stuck with orange, red and flame.
But you can pick from seven shades –
no other season's quite the same.

And as for all my winter groups,
my goodness, they would envy you
with all the colours you can paint –
far more than they could ever do!

So take a chair, pick up your brush
and let's get started straight away!
What greater pleasure could there be
than painting a fine summer's day?'

The earth does not argue.

'A song of the rolling earth' by Walt Whitman (1819-92)

Earth doesn't argue. That's true, but plants do.
That's if the earth is not treated by you.
Earth may be passive. What's in it is not.
Earth doesn't argue but plants can – a lot!

Earth doesn't argue, but does need a feed,
and plants within it will say what they need.
Earth doesn't argue, but plants can – a lot.
Passive? Accepting? No, certainly not.

The true genius is a mind of large general powers, accidentally turned to some particular direction.

Samuel Johnson (1709-84)

Genius – for me – robotic mowers
that save us gardeners countless boring hours,
turned to each particular direction,
seemingly endowed with magic powers.
Accidentally turned? No, never, ever,
and never going to the same place twice.
Wonderful! But sadly, so expensive.
True genius – but goodness, at a price!

Behold the child, by nature's kindly law,
Pleased with a rattle, tickled with a straw.

'An Essay on Man' by Alexander Pope (1688-1744)

Behold the child, too, who likes even more
to go out with you through the garden door
and plays there happily for many hours,
and enjoys it – watering the flowers.
Behold the child, by nature's kindly law,
one day to be a gardener – for sure!

The love of money is the root of all evil

1 Timothy 6.10

Love of plants – the root of overspending,
since what they cost today can be quite daft.
Luckily, I have a small town garden,
or else I'd have a massive overdraft!

A love of plants – the root of penury.
And while they grow, our bank accounts do not.
Even a small patch – like my own garden –
can see our savings going down a lot.

Easy to spend trolley-loads of money –
it's terrifying what we pay today,
but with all those gems in garden centres,
it's ever harder keeping well away!

All really grim gardeners possess a keen sense of humus.

Garden rubbish by W.C. Sellar (1898-1951) and R.J. Yeatman (1897-1968)

You're right, as it's the gardener's gold –
not one could live without this mould.
But why say only *grim* ones do?
We happy gardeners use it too!

We're all the happier for it –
it's good soul food for gardeners too.
Grim-faced? We're quite the opposite!
Did that not strike the two of you?

I am not a dirt gardener – I sit with my walking stick and point out things that need to be done.

Sir Edwin Hardy Amies (1909-2003)

My God, that must have cost a bomb!
Sit back? Let others do the lot?
You must have had a goodly stash
to draw out of your pension pot!
Your stick suggests a certain age,
and possibly you lived alone
and had to get in gardeners
for jobs you couldn't do alone.
But getting dirty, down to earth –
now, *that's* more like the real thing!
Dirt's always at the core of it,
right at the heart of gardening.
Dirt on hands and round our faces
and twigs and leaves caught up in hair,
and nails that need a damned good scrub
and clothes with scuff marks everywhere.
A messy job is gardening,
so maybe it is no surprise
that many simply delegate,
and only want to use their eyes.
Like you, they only point out things –
and then let others do them too.
But wasn't it much less reward
when who had done them wasn't you?

The more help a man has in his garden, the less it belongs to him.

W.H. Davies (1871-1940)

Ah, someone who agrees with me,
but put it far more wittily!

Sometimes I sits and thinks. And then again I just sits.

Punch magazine

Ah, you're like me. I sit and think.
And then again, I simply sit.
It's often when my brain's gone blank
that sudden thoughts rush into it.
Sitting outside in the garden
and pondering, not wandering,
is often when plans come to me
and good ideas for gardening.

If music be the food of love, play on.

Twelfth Night by William Shakespeare (1564-1616)

Do our plants respond to music?
It's very often said they do,
and when I play them opera
I tend to think it may be true.

Callas floating through the garden –
I like to think helps flowers grow.
But does it? Maybe fanciful.
There's no way I will ever know.

Does music really help them on?
Or, more likely, fertiliser?
No way, of course, of finding out.
Using both, I'm none the wiser!

No verse can give pleasure for long, nor last, that is written in sobriety.

Epistles *by Horace, (65 BC-8 BC)*

Thanks, Horace! Then there's hope for me –
a fan of the odd G and T
and rosé – that's my favourite drink –
the best in summertime, I think.

No verse gives pleasure that you know
if penned while drinking H2O?
Well, Horace, you have made my day –
a truly lovely thing to say!

I think a drink from time to time
(as you do) maybe aids one's rhyme –
as gardens do with poetry –
at least, I like that theory.

But mad it is to write too sloshed,
a surefire way to know we've boshed.
We read the words penned yesterday,
appalled, and chuck them all away.

How many poems doomed by drink?
Quite probably a lot, I think.
But not to drink a single drop?
No! Creativity might stop!

Heaven – I'm in heaven and my heart beats so that I can hardly speak.

Irving Berlin (1888 -1989)

Heaven – I'm in heaven –
as I've been out gardening every day this week,
where I always find the happiness I seek,
if the weather doesn't turn too grey and bleak!

Heaven – I'm in heaven –
for the sun's been shining every single day,
and there's not one thing that's keeping me away,
and the forecast's good as well. Hip, hip, hooray!

Heaven – I'm in heaven –
when the skies above are always brilliant blue;
not a drop of rain, and for the whole week through.
How I love a week like that! I'm sure, like you!

Did God who gave us flowers and trees also provide the allergies?

'A nose is a nose is a nose' by E.Y.Harburg (1896-1981)

Did God give us the allergies?
Yes, I suppose – God only knows.
But if he did, how strange of him
to so afflict the eyes and nose!

Did God give us the allergies?
I rather think he must have done;
but why afflict us gardeners
and make our outside days less fun?

Streaming tears and nasty rashes –
that hardly makes for happy days.

But then God is a funny chap.
He never ceases to amaze!

Perhaps he gave us allergies
in order to protect the plants
and stop us humans touching them,
and give their lives a better chance.

Study nature, love nature, stay close to nature. It will never fail you.

Frank Lloyd Wright (1867-1959)

What? Never fail you, Frank Lloyd Wright?
I'd love to know what plants you grew!
A fail-safe plot? Impossible?
They *can't* have been that kind to you!

Soul first, soil next

Soul first, soil next –
wise words, that text.
Soul one, soil two –
so true, so true.
No soul, no chance –
first rule with plants.
Weak soil – plants know.
Most types won't grow.
Soul first, good start.
First part, shows heart.
Then soil, good soil –
worth work, worth toil.
Bad soil, no soul –
own goal, own goal!

The bookcase

Wow, all your lovely gardening books!
But just how many do you need?
And, if you are truly honest,
how many do you ever read?

Shiny covers, pristine pages,
not one well-thumbed as it should be.
Birthday presents, Christmas presents –
but dusty, the majority!

Gardeners – often given books
(by other gardeners, frequently)
who'll also have an overload.
Now, time to give to charity?

Television contracts the imagination, and radio expands it.

Sir Terry Wogan (1938-2016)

No, not if it's a garden show,
and not if we can't see the plants.
It's then that television shows
give gardeners a better chance.
For questions, radio is fine.
It's then that we don't need to see.
But if we want to *picture* things,
then radio can't beat T.V.!

Oh, how many torments lie in the small circle of a wedding ring!

The Double Gallant by Colley Cibber (1671-1757)

But oh, how many pleasures lie
in that small circle of a ring
when husbands love to see us out,
and so contented gardening!
And even greater pleasures lie
within the circle of a ring
when partners are encouraging,
though gardening is not their thing!

You can never plan the future from the past.

Edmund Burke (1729-97)

That's something all we gardeners do
while learning from each past mistake,
taking care we don't repeat them.
So what a strange remark to make!
Moreover, how can humans plan
without referring to the past
and what worked well and what did not,
and also learning from that – fast?

The guest from hell

He plonked himself upon a chair
and drank for hours and hours,
and never ever commented
on any plants and flowers.
He helped himself to loads of booze
and never wandered round,
and then, when I suggested that,
the fellow stood his ground.

I don't expect a compliment,
or people to love flowers,
but, still, I think it's rude to sit
in gardens many hours
without a single look at them –
not even one quick glance –
in fact, not even *noticing*
the many flowers and plants!

If at first you don't succeed, try, try again

The rhododendron hates my soil,
even though it's quite well treated.
But one is perfect – in a tub.
And this time I am not defeated.

Your soil is much too alkaline?
For many of us, there's the rub.
But why not buy a baby one
and grow it in a garden tub?

I fed mine with peaty compost,
and, goodness me, before I knew
the rhododendron flowered for me.
Amazing just how fast it grew!

Just plant your baby out in March,
and then, if it's at all like mine,
you'll find that it will love its tub.
With peat to eat, you'll find it's fine!

Anything you can do, I can do better.

'Annie get your gun' by Irving Berlin (1888 -1989)

Any jobs I can do, *you* can do better,
like fixing the mower or mending the rake.
Practically everyone does those jobs better,
and does them in less time than I'd ever take.
Anything I can do, you can do better,
and lots of things you can do, I simply can't.
We gardeners aren't always practical people,
and I'm pretty good proof that some gardeners aren't!

Praise where praise is due

Every year I think my summer garden
looks better than it did the year before,
though I know the people who come over
may see no difference through the garden door.
Some of them may notice it looks pretty
and maybe say so over welcome drinks.
Best to shrug it off if they say nothing
and not to care what anybody thinks.
Garden for yourself or other people?
I think most gardeners fall between the two,
loving it when someone in the garden
rewards us with kind words when praise is due!

The grinding of the intellect is for most people as painful as a dentist's drill.

Leonard Woolf (1880-1969)

Especially when in the garden
when people grind on – and for hours
without so much as one quick glance
at any of our plants and flowers.

The grinding of the intellect –
that's fine, but not at lunch outside
if no-one bothers looking round
at what has given us such pride.

The grinding of the intellect –
yes, painful as a dentist's drill,
especially at lunch outside
and with an afternoon to kill!

The grinding of the intellect –
of course there is a place for it.
But how much nicer it would be
if lunch guests strolled around a bit!

Order! Order!

'A garden needs strict order', said my dad.
I always found his way of thinking sad.
A soldier, he preferred an ordered space.
Unruliness he simply couldn't face.

For plants, it was strict discipline – or out.
No stragglers, slackers were allowed about.
In spring, the borders – just like a brigade –
all bright-red tulips, as if on parade.

A rambling rose, deserting from its post,
soon got hacked back to three feet at the most.
Young plants, lined up like cadets on duty.
Their *behaviour* noted, not their beauty.

Perhaps that's why I love a wilderness.
Last thing I want out there is tidiness.
I like it when the plants are free to roam,
and where, I like to think, they feel at home;
not strictly ordered, cut back and confined,
and owned by someone whom they find is kind.

That's why the lady is a tramp.

Lorenz Hart (1895-1943)

Because she gardens? Mostly fails
to paint her face, or else her nails?
Because she rarely wears a dress?
In jeans the mud will matter less.
Because she never wears high heels,
as not one gardener ever kneels
in smart shoes with stilettos on?
Because chic clothes she'd rarely don?
We gardeners can be tramps – me too.
We often look a mess – that's true!

In sickness and in health

Food that costs nothing –
always appealing,
but wild cress I'd leave well alone.
'Fluke' may be present,
highly unpleasant,
as records have constantly shown.

Lethal to cattle,
risky for people
(unlike cress commercially grown).
Fluke attacks livers;
gives me the shivers.
The dangers should be better known.

Cress by fast rivers –
safer for livers,
but not where the water is still.
Fine when it's growing
where it's fast-flowing.
If not, there's a chance it may kill.

Cress – quite delicious,
also pernicious
for walkers who don't know that fact,
and never would guess
that waterside cress
might well get their livers attacked.

But if you *must* pick,
boiling's the best trick.
That should nuke the fluke, so it's said.
Add stock to the gloop,
then cream to make soup.
With luck, you won't end up in bed.

Still, I'd be wary.
Wild cress is scary.
Why pick it, and lose any sleep?
Please don't unearth it,
just isn't worth it,
especially when bought cress is cheap!

Plants form no opinions about their caregivers

What balderdash! Of course they do.
Plants often grumble and complain,
and take a view (and dim ones, too)
and make their feelings pretty plain.

What? No opinions? Are you blind?
Have you not seen a wilting plant
that says you ought to water it?
A gardener, you clearly aren't!

No clear feedback? No harsh judgements?
Plants air opinions pretty fast.
And have you not seen grumblers there
in any plants you're walking past?

They wilt. You haven't noticed that?
They're pretty quick to criticise.
You need new glasses urgently.
There's something faulty with your eyes!

A problem shared is a problem halved

Fed up with a bolting lettuce?
Just dig it up, then plant again.
The lettuce won't like that at all.
What's more, it makes its feelings plain.

It's shocked, and needs to rest for days.
The last thing it can do is grow.
And bolt it can't, not any more –
a tip I learned some years ago.

All lettuces when shooting off
taste too bitter, quite revolting.
So there you are – a useful tip
next time noticing they're bolting!

If you think squash is a competitive activity, try flower-arranging.

Alan Bennett (1934 -)

Flower-arranging competitions
can sometimes make me feel quite old.
Arrangements made with man-made things
are often those that scoop the gold.

Steel and string and raffia –
all muddled up with gorgeous plants.
And those who hate that (as I do)
won't win a cup. There's not a chance.

Things have to change, of course they do.
We all need to experiment.
But things have now gone much too far
inside the flower arrangement tent.

And entrants – *so* competitive.
Arrangers – not a passive breed
(as Alan Bennett rightly says).
That's something else I just don't need.

Flower-arranging, now like warfare,
and winners – warriors today.
Would I enter competitions?
Not any more. I stay away!

The French and the English are divided by a lot more than a strip of sea

Like many people, I grow mint.
And so, I'm pretty sure, do you.
What's more, I'd never serve up lamb
without at least a sprig or two.

And yes, of course I'll make a sauce –
it goes with lamb so perfectly,
although the French would not agree,
they'd see that as a travesty.

Mint with lamb – to Brits, delicious,
and mint with spuds, that's hard to beat,
but if you have a Gallic nose,
two dishes that you'd *never* eat.

Serve mint with meat? 'Non. Dégoûlasse!'
And mint with spuds? 'C'est barbarie!'
Our two nations are divided
by far more than a strip of sea.

A mint patch – here a common sight,
but not in 'potagers' in France.
And as for serving lamb with mint,
across the Channel, not a chance!

Nothing is more pleasant to the eye than green grass kept finely shorn.

'Of Gardens' by Francis Bacon (1561-1626)

Oh, one thing is – your old man mowing it,
without you asking him to do his bit!
More pleasant to the eye is green grass shorn
when someone *else* has gone and mown the lawn!

Out of sight, out of mind

I know where sweet peas want to be.
That's anywhere they can't see me.
Always failures, as are dahlias.
They find my place a misery.

Right out of sight and out of mind –
that's where they all want *me* to be.
Oh, why do plants give up on me
and so infuriatingly?

I have spread my dreams under your feet.

'The Cloths of Heaven' by W.B.Yeats (1865-1939)

I've just discovered ancient Greeks
were passionate about their roses,
though not in vases round the house
or else to tie in lovers' posies.

They loved to strew the petals round –
thick carpets of them in the hall –
to show the guests how rich they were
and thoroughly impress them all.

The thicker the rose carpets were,
the more the guests would be impressed,
especially if the scented spread
(when crushed), was instantly refreshed.

The ladies all adored those carpets
of petals underneath their feet,
and no doubt also loved a chap
as rich as Croesus; great to meet!

A hall awash with scented petals?
Oh, *how* romantic that would be!
I rather think the ancient Greeks
might well have had their way with me!

Weeds are not supposed to grow,
but by degrees.
Some achieve a flower,
though no-one sees.

'Modesties' by Philip Larkin (1922-85)

Of course we see the flowers weeds will sprout,
like orange ones when dandelions are out.
Quite clearly, Larkin, gardener you were not.
It's hard to think of any hue more hot!

Seems to me you needed better glasses.
I'm sorry if that makes me sound unkind.
But it's mad to stroll around a garden
(or anywhere at all) if you're half-blind!

Of course, I'm an optimist. I don't see the point of being anything else.

Sir Winston Churchill (1874-1965)

Nothing to do inside.
Nothing at all – what bliss!
No one to see all day
and no one that I'll miss.

Nothing to buy at all.
I bought it yesterday.
Nobody dropping in.
Nobody here to stay.

No one I have to phone.
Nothing I have to pay.
Nowhere to go but out.
Nothing to spoil my day.

Nothing and no one – great.
No, nothing on my plate.
Nothing but gardening.
What bliss! I just can't wait!

You never get a second chance to make a first impression.

Walter Margulies (1914-85)

Four days of painting flowers,
and right round our front door.
A note to darling Sydney –
we couldn't thank you more.

And what a lovely welcome
we now have for each guest!
Thanks, Sydney Sykes, friend, artist –
all guests come in, impressed.

A sign of instant welcome –
just what a door is for.
A flower-painted door frame?
If only we saw more!

Don't expect everyone to love gardening!

'Fancy looking round the garden?'
'No, sorry Liz. No, not a lot.
Mind if I look round the cupboard
and see what brand of Scotch you've got?'

'Sure! Pour a glass, and then come out!'
'Er, no. I'd rather drink it here.'
Quite clearly, I'm a garden bore.
He's made that clear. Oh dear, oh dear!

It might or might not be right to kill, but sometimes it is necessary.

'Before the dawn' by Gerry Adams (1948-)

Gardeners, all, are not just growers.
We're also killers, that is true.
Which of us has never pruned?
It's necessary, so we do.
When chopping back the older growth
a surge of guilt runs through my head,
and pruning's something I dislike –
selecting what will soon be dead.
It might, or might not be right
to kill, but we gardeners do.
However odd, we all play God
while killing old growth for the new.

I think of a pessimist as someone waiting for it to rain.

Leonard Cohen (1934-2016

You clearly knew no gardeners.
In summertime we long for rain
to come and drench the sun-baked earth,
to hose again is such a pain.
Unravelling the garden hose
and coiling it back up again
is always such a boring task.
We're optimistic it will rain!
And sprinklers left on all day long
will double up the water bill,
although we do exactly that
as days of drought can quickly kill.
All optimists we gardeners are
in every single bout of drought,
and pessimists we're clearly not,
as Leonard should have thought about!

Procrastination is the thief of time.

Edward Young (1683-1765)

So true, and it's the thief of many plants –
the ones we should have tended, but did not.
Now lost, because we've been away too long,
or didn't water when it got too hot.

Procrastination means the death of many plants
that cannot wait, alas, for TLC.
Too much delay and many pass away.
A form of unintended cruelty.

Procrastination is the thief of time,
and thief of plants we should have watered more.
How sad it is, when we're returning home,
to find a desert right outside the door.

The kind of people who always go on about whether a thing is good taste invariably have very bad taste.

Joe Orton (1933-1967)

Rarely do I think of taste in gardens,
except when spotting frightful garden gnomes.
Why do people have these ghastly objects?
Such eyesores round their gardens and their homes!

So now I know, Joe, *I* have rotten taste –
and lots of other gardeners just like me –
thousands, maybe millions of gnome-haters
who see each one as a monstrosity!

All gardening is landscape painting.

Joseph Spence Anecdotes *by Alexander Pope (1688-1744)*

A lovely thought. Am I a painter too?
I love to think that I can do the two.
Oh, how uplifting that is for the mind –
imagining the two are intertwined!

Gardeners' recipe – one part soil, two parts water, and three parts wishful thinking

One part soil and two parts water,
and three parts wishful thinking, sure.
And one of those is sometimes wishing
our friends would notice rather more.

Ours can be a lonely hobby
which friends and partners do not share,
simply not that interested
in anything we grow out there.

Gardeners, driven by our own thing,
might find our passion far more fun
if others showed a bit more interest
in what, exactly, we have done!

No furniture so charming as books.

A Memoir of the Reverend Sydney Smith *(1771-1845),*

'Please, girls, don't bring your home-made jam
or any chutneys that you've made,

and don't bring any strawberries
or any home-made marmalade.
Don't bring apples, don't bring cherries
or lettuces or beans or leeks,
or any other vegetables –
we've got enough to last for weeks.
Please *don't* bring any home-made stuff;
just you, your book and nothing more.
A *book club* we're supposed to be,
and *not* the local produce store!'

Today the problem that has no name is how to juggle work, love, home and children.

The Second Stage *by Betty Friedan (1921-2006)*

And gardens too – you left that out,
the first thing that will go to pot
with so much else upon our plates.
Fifth burden in a woman's lot!

Don't have a garden? Possible.
But where are all the kids to play?
The last place most mums want their kids
is underneath their feet all day.

Today the problem with no name
is how to juggle everything.
With work and love and home and kids,
first thing to go is gardening.

There's no point in looking back

Dock – something we all used to know,
and for its leaves, but not its petals –
such brilliant doctors were those leaves
when badly stung by stinging nettles.

No better antidote for stings,
but now a plant few children see –
and more's the pity, stuck at home
and watching a new DVD.

And would they even know the nettle,
or ever go where nettles grow?
At least kids wouldn't need the dock
as children used to years ago.

Memories are made of this.

Terry Gilkyson, Richard Dehr and Frank Miller, sung by Dean Martin

A piece of garden statuary
can make a lovely wedding gift
when couples have a spot outside.
To pass one brings an instant lift.

I have one in my garden here –
a cherub with a lyre to play –
and every time I pass him by
I think about my wedding day.

And when the days are cold and grey
he seems to play his lyre to me.
I float back to my wedding day,
remembering the gaiety.

I see my cherub on the steps,
the day floats back, each memory.
I hear the laughter once again.
My cherub brings it back to me.

With many thanks to my sister Sally-Jane and her husband Bryan for their marvellous present all those years ago

He who's afraid of every nettle should not piss in the grass.

Reverend Thomas Fuller (1608-61)

'Devil's Plaything',
'Common nettle',
'Hokey Pokey',
'Jimmy Nettle' –
so many names our nettles have,
but only one on which I'd settle.
'Stinging nettles' – accurate,
as sting is what all nettles do.
I'd never use the other names,
though country people often do.
My runner-up is 'Devil's Plaything',
as devilish its stings can be,
and getting stung when I was young
remains a painful memory.
'Those afraid of stinging nettles
should never piss when in the grass.'
I wish our teachers had said that
to kids in Nature Study class!

When life gives you lemons, make a gin and tonic

Are gardeners mostly optimistic?
I tend to think the answer's yes.
Out there, the problems fade away
or often seem to matter less.

When life brings lemons, we make gin
and wander off outside again.
Quite suddenly, life's not too bad.
We see the sunshine, not the rain.

Women never have young minds. They are born a thousand years old.

A Taste of Honey *by Shelagh Delaney (1938-2011)*

Women never have young minds?
My garden-loving friends all do –
all keeping minds alert and young
while busy out there all year through,
and joining all the fun and games
when grandchildren are there to stay.
What? 'Women never have young minds.'
That's quite the oddest thing to say!'

Can I have a bit of earth?

The Secret Garden *by Frances Hodgson Burnett (1849-1924)*

'Can I have a bit of earth?' asked Mary.
And 'Can I have a bit of earth?' asked I.
Both of us were luckily rewarded,
and gardeners we became. That's surely why.

'Can I have a bit of earth?' kids ask us.
But where, if we don't have an outside space?
Window boxes are the perfect answer.
They'll put a smile upon a youngster's face!

Plants can plant a love of them for lifetimes,
a gift that's very often left unsung,
and the best time they can ever do that
is early on, and when we're very young.

I am a sundial, and I make a botch of what is done much better by a watch.

Ogden Nash (1902-71)

'I am a watch, and always know the time.
But then, my beauty is far less sublime.
You have a timeless charm; all dials do.
I often wish I'd been made more like you.'

One is nearer God's heart in a garden than anywhere else on earth.

Dorothy Frances Gurney (1858-1932)

And we're nearer to *broke* in a garden –
planting one out costs the earth!

It was such a lovely day – I thought it was a pity to get up.

Somerset Maugham (1874-1965)

No gardener then, was Somerset.
No gardener was he.
No gardener could stay in bed,
or not for long – like me!

We boil at different degrees.

'Society and Solitude' by Ralph Waldo Emerson (1803-82)

Ever met an angry person
whose main pursuit is gardening?
All gardens calm their owners down
and tempers are the rarest thing.
I know of not one gardener
who's ever boiled or lost the plot.
We don't all boil, or boil at all.
Bad-tempered? Gardeners? I think not!

Greater love hath no man than this

John 15.13

What woman in her rightful mind
would give up half her garden space
to build a model railway room
and still possess a smiling face?

Er, me. No greater sign of love
can woman ever give her spouse
than giving half the garden up
to build a railway in the house.

Two hobbies do not always mix,
there has to be a compromise.
There was – the railway room was built,
and now I'm thrilled, to my surprise.

In fact, it's turned out very well.
I quickly found the railway fun,
and if some garden hadn't gone,
I think my husband might have done!

He plays with trains while I'm outside.
What's more I like to hear him laugh
when trains go round without a hitch.
At least I've kept my other half!

Goodbye to all that.

Robert Graves (1885-1985)

Goodbye summer, far less blooming,
though skies are still a pleasant blue.
Hello autumn, here too soon,
but still I'll try and welcome you.

Lots and lots of compensations,
like walking in a gorgeous wood.
But in my garden, autumn, *please*,
keep leaves on longer if you could!

The devil is in the detail

The angel's in the detail with every growing thing.
Miraculous, those details we notice gardening.
So intricate, so complex, a botanist's delight.
(The other job I thought of before I chose to write).
The angel's in the detail, the devil clearly not,
explaining to me sometimes what drops of faith I've got.

III

‘Mists and mellow fruitfulness’
‘Ode to Autumn’ by John Keats

Autumn

I never see a flower that pleases me, but I wish for you.

William Wordsworth (1770-1850)

That almost brings a tear into my eye.
I'd *love* that said to me before I die!
But just how many flowers did you see
and tell yourself each time 'That pleases me'.
You must have wished for her a thousand times.
How did you find the time to write your rhymes?

You never saw a flower that pleased you so,
without a wish that she would never go?
Not once or twice? You surely must have done!
You thought of her with *every single one*?
Ah, so romantic, Wordsworth – what a line!
And what a husband – not at all like mine!

There is no greater pain than to remember a happy time when one is in misery.

Divina Commedia *by Dante Alighieri (1265-1321)*

Dear Dante, I so disagree.
To me, it's just the opposite.
Remembering a happy time
can ease one's pain – and quite a bit.
And memories of days gardening
can soothe me most effectively.
In fact, my garden is, to me,
the *enemy* of misery.

Ignorance is bliss.

Thomas Gray (1716-71)

A lot of gardeners that I know
don't know the names of plants they grow.
They buy a new variety
and then forget the name, like me.

We should have left the label on,
but didn't, and the name has gone.
And what's more (this bit's rather nice)
we also can't recall the price.

Then, not remembering the cost
soon makes up for the name that's lost,
especially if the plant's a hit
and more than worth the price of it.

Forgetting people's names – that's bad.
Forgetting plant names much less sad.
And quite forgetting what we paid
is brilliant news – our day is made!

It's time you turned over a new leaf

I wish my old horse chestnut would.
Now every leaf is spotted brown.
Like all these trees, with mite disease,
though I can't bear to chop it down.

Autumn blues

'Gosh I'm fed up with the garden,
a ton more leaves to clear each day.
Let's piss off somewhere nice abroad,
and have a decent holiday!

I'm sick and tired of clearing them
and driving to the council skip.'
'I know, but you'll find millions more
the day we get back from the trip.'

Brexit

Will that mean less Polish gardeners?
Will that affect the price of flowers?
Yes, probably – let's wait and see,
not bore our gardening friends for hours.

All sorts of things could soon be banned,
and imports might well take a hit
when left to wilt when at crowded docks.
And that won't be the end of it.

Good teachers make the best of a pupil's means – great teachers foresee a pupil's ends.

Maria Callas (1923-77)

'Now, paint in colours bright and bold,
ignore the softer shades, young man.
Choose shades like reds and oranges.
My autumn students always can.

Pick up your brush and go for it!
Ah, scarlet, that's the perfect hue.
And don't forget that autumn skies
can often be a brilliant blue.

Burnt umber? Great – a perfect choice.
Bright yellow – *good* – you're learning fast!
I think you'll paint a masterpiece
before the autumn months have passed.

And gold – that's splendid, big and bold;
the perfect choice for many trees.
But let's have lots more falling leaves
and plenty wind-tossed in the breeze.

You should do well here in my class,
that's if you take advice from me.
Remember, autumn shades are *hot*,
and bolder yours should always be.'

A great lesson in life

Watching kids pick blackberries –
illuminating, always true.
Just hand each one a plastic bag
and then watch out for what they do.
Some will pick and never eat one,
while others eat half those they pick,
or end up eating all of them
until they cough up purple sick.

Watching kids pick blackberries
is almost most enlightening.
It shows how different they are.
I've always found it interesting.
You notice who's competitive
and other children who are not –
all kinds of tiny little things
that show the characters they've got.

Some work like demons picking them
while others don't, and soon lose heart –
miffed to see the quicker pickers.
The children can be poles apart.
You spot dissenters – also true,
the ones who quickly go on strike
and hide behind a blackberry bush
and find the whole darned thing a hike.

You notice who gets into it
or out of it in minutes flat,
staring round at other children –
you very often notice that.
You spot the future freelancers –
the ones who strike out on their own
and do not like to work in teams
and maybe won't when fully grown.

You see the more adventurous
who work at greater distances

or higher up into the bush,
however dangerous that is.
So many little clues are there
about their personalities.
A fascinating exercise
is watching kids pick blackberries!

Sweet day, so cool, so calm, so bright,
the bridal of the earth and sky:
the dew shall weep thy fall tonight,
for thou must die.

George Herbert (1593-1633)

Dull day today – so cold, so grey,
no sun above me, only rain.
Depresses me, I have to say: a bloody pain.

Dull day, what's more, it's Saturday
with lots of things outside to do.
I wish the rain would go away. It won't; that's true.

Dull day, that's what the forecast said,
and sadly, this time they were right.
And worse, they forecast solid rain until tonight.

And Sunday will be rainy too.
A bloody washout, this weekend.
The only place where I will go is round the bend.

Only a sweet and virtuous soul
could stand a wet weekend like this.
It makes my soul as black as coal. It's one I'd miss!

Gardening is nature's way of telling you you're getting older

Age, do not wither us, nor old bones stale
and steal last drops of gardening energy.
Age, please do not condemn us all indoors
away from where we gardeners want to be.

Age, do not force us to put down our forks
until the last. For that, we gardeners pray.
Whatever else you choose to do with us,
make our last day the one we're forced away.

Age, if you must, add wrinkles, ever more,
and backs that ache when lifting up the spade,
but let us, 'til the last, enjoy outside
and never let our lifelong passion fade.

Age, leave us pride and let us go outside
and wander as we always used to do,
with sticks, maybe, to marvel at our plants
until our final day of life is through.

Age, pity us, and pity too the plants
that loved us for our tender, loving care.
Think about us all, and 'ere we've gone
and how our plants will cope without us there.

Age, please be kind and let us go outside
and wander as we always used to do,
with aids, perhaps, and maybe fearful steps
until our final day of life is through.

Rotten luck

Today, in gardens, rot is hot –
the rusting chair, the ancient pot.
And lots of things receive more praise
than once they did in younger days.
We tend to like things past their prime
reminding us of passing time.
Now age is trendy, youth is not –
at least, within a garden plot.
The sun-bleached gate, the mildewed wall –
we do not mind the rot at all.
The wooden table, faded white,
the wrought iron, once as black as night.
We love age showing in the place,
but still not in the human face.
Obsessed with looking ever young,
the signs of age are still unsung.
How sad, in gardens, age is hot,
but in a human face, it's not.

Know when to back off!

Don't pull roots after sixty plus.
Get someone younger, my advice.
Slipped discs, not the greatest feeling.
And if you *must* pull, pay the price!

Chiropractic beds that drop
to try and realign your spine –
not the greatest fun or feeling.
I know. And so do friends of mine!

Gardeners – loved by chiropractors.
So leave those wretched roots alone.
Get someone young to pull them out,
and *never* pull them on your own!

Nature, Mr Allnut, is what we are put into this world to rise above.

The African Queen *by James Agee (1909-55)*

Or look up to, surely, Agee,
and make us marvel at what's there,
and rise above it – that we can't,
or shouldn't with the wonders there.
Man's nature we should rise above –
I know that thought was in your mind,
but nature in a garden space
is inspirational, I find.
Mother Nature, Mr Agee,
is what we *shouldn't* rise above.
It's surely there to comfort us
and give us something else to love.

Better safe than sorry

Trampolines for children's parties.
A wooden house up in a tree.
Firework parties in the garden.
Quite soon, they'll all be history.
And conker matches, garden ponds –
both safety issues now, a shame.
Costs a bomb to get insurance,
but accidents – and you're to blame.

Remember when you climbed up trees
and waved to parents at the top?
Challenges we loved to tackle
have mostly, sadly, had to stop.
And penknives – now a rarity,
or only used with parents there.
Freedoms that we took for granted
have largely gone, to my despair.

Gone are toys like bows and arrows.
It very often makes me sigh.
Instead, it's all computer games.
The world outside has passed kids by.
A safer one, but sorrier –
cocooned, our children nowadays –
more likely to reach adulthood,
but missing out in many ways.

Safer plonked in front of telly
where parents know just where they are,
though wondering and frequently,
if everything has gone too far.
'Health and Safety' – taking over.
A safer world, a better one?
Of course it is in certain ways,
though some would say a lot less fun.

Time spent outside? More spent inside –
and far, far more than once was true.
Shove the kids out in the garden?
No, not like parents used to do.
Frost or snow, we got shoved out,
though not when it was pouring rain.
But those days won't be coming back.
We won't be seeing them again.

An old chestnut

Extremely rude to chestnut trees.
The strangest phrase, it seems to me.
Chestnuts – gorgeous and delicious,
with many uses culinary.
One of autumn's great delights –
the fruits of a great chestnut tree.
So how did *that* phrase come about?
An irritating mystery.

If you go down to the woods today, you're sure of a big surprise.

'The Teddy Bears' Picnic' by Jimmy Kennedy (1902-84)

If you go down to the woods today,
you're sure of a big surprise.
So many trees are sick today,
you may not believe your eyes.
And every kind that ever there was
may not survive for certain, because
today's the day disease is having a picnic.

If you go out in the woods today,
you'll notice some new disease.
It's so, so sad in the woods today,
we're losing too many trees.
And every type that ever there was
may not survive for ever, because
disease in trees is truly having a picnic.

The morning after the night before

When kitchens shout, 'PLEASE CLEAN ME UP!'
(that's when you've had eight to dinner)
and gardens whisper, 'Please come out!'
who do you find is the winner?

Gardens I find more persuasive
than any indoor space can be.
No matter what the mess inside,
I'll wander out – and instantly!

If you've got a bad back, back off!

Back pain – such a common problem,
and something older gardeners dread.
Give yourself a decent mattress,
and give your plants a raised-up bed.
Yes, beds like that are quite expensive,
(but chiropractors are as well)
and leaning over flowerbeds
is no fun when the pain is hell.
Plants do well in raised-up beds,
exactly as we humans do.
Less pests for them, less aches for us.
Your spine will soon be thanking you!

Our autumn years

When the spade is getting hard to handle,
the day the fork's becoming quite a strain,
is not the day to give up gardening,
it's just the one to pause and think again.

Things like raised-up beds could be the answer,
or helpers who don't charge too much an hour,
or lighter tools, made for older people,
and plants that need a lot less help to flower.

When the fork and spade are hard to manage,
it's not the time to stop. Good heavens, no!
Just the time to pause and think things over,
and maybe think of simpler plants to grow.

IV

'Blow, blow, thy winter wind.'
'As you like it' by William Shakespeare

Winter

O, Wind,
if winter comes, can spring be far behind?

'Ode to the West Wind' by Percy Bysshe Shelley (1792-1822)

O, yes,
she can be far behind.
Spring's often very late.
She knows exactly when to come,
but then forgets the date.
Her memory is terrible.
Latecomer, that is she.
There's one word that she doesn't know.
Which? Punctuality.

O, yes.
she can be weeks behind
and rarely seems to care
that we become frustrated souls
with little growing there.
She doesn't keep a calendar.
That's simply not her way.
She *will* arrive, eventually,
but she will pick her day.

You're only given a little spark of madness.
You mustn't lose it.

Robin Williams (1951-2014)

Brrr! Freezing out there! Horrible!
What am I doing pottering,
a fur around my dressing gown
and half-blind, both eyes watering?
Brrr! Icy out here, bloody cold,
my hands around a mug of tea.
What *am* I doing out first thing?

Is anyone as mad as me?
God gives us one spark of madness.
We mustn't lose it – that is true.
But should I freeze to death outside?
Is that what other gardeners do?

A round robin

A robin, puffed to twice its size.
A ball of feathers, watching me,
waiting for a crumb of comfort
to ease his winter misery.
A round, round, robin, miserable
and longing, longing for the spring –
as I am, getting through the days
without one day out gardening.

The big sleep.

Raymond Chandler (1888-1959)

Far from dead, our Mother Earth is sleeping
(and often oversleeping, in my view).
Nothing we can do will ever wake her.
We have to wait until the sun peeps through.
Only sun can stir her, like Prince Charming.
The Prince of Light is always who's to blame –
a sleepyhead himself, as bad as earth is –
all we can do is play a waiting game.

A perpetual holiday is a working definition of hell.

Parents and Children *by George Bernard Shaw (1856-1950)*

Something to get up for every day –
a blessing when that something is outside.
A holiday ahead for many years?
Like Shaw, that's something I could not abide.
Thank God for gardens giving us more work
when at the age we're out of offices,
with something there to keep us occupied.
A constant holiday? How sad that is!

The time is not remote when I
must by the course of nature die.

'Verses on the death of Dr Swift' by Jonathan Swift (1667-1745)

The time is not remote when I
must by the course of nature die,
but still, I hope to die in bed,
not gardening outside instead.
How easy 'tis to fall and trip
down steps, or on a wet lawn slip,
and break our ankles, fracture knees,
or fall from ladders, pruning trees!
Gardener's World on television
makes us risk our lives and vision;
we try and do the same as they,
disaster's never far away.
We try and master all their tricks,
then poke our eyes on bamboo sticks,
and lug big sacks with ghastly risks
of pulling muscles, slipping discs.
How many fall, do you suppose,
forgetting where we've left the hose?

How many of us lose our toes
when using Flymos? God, who knows?
How many of us move a pot,
forgetting that our backs are not
equipped with the right vertebrae
to lift them up that easily?
The time is not remote when I
must by the course of nature die.
But still, I hope to die in bed,
not gardening outside instead!

Pushing up the daisies

'Pushing up the daisies'–
a marvellous turn of phrase.
I like to think I'll do that
when I have passed my days.
I owe it to the daisies,
as when I ever mow,
I flatten them in dozens,
and have, since years ago.
I'd rather like to help them,
the least that I can do,
for all those years of mowing.
A thank-you will be due.

True guilt is, the obligation one owes oneself to be oneself.

The Self and Others *by R.D. Laing (1927-89)*

True guilt, I think, is wishing time away
until I see those first green shoots of spring,
and loathing frosts and zero temperatures
which stop me going outside now first thing.
Season of snow – a winter wonderland,
so different now from only weeks ago.
Season of ice – a frozen fairyland,
but outside now, I do not want to go.
Season of red berries on my holly,
the only jolly colour to bring cheer.
And time of guilt for wishing it away
while waiting for the spring to reappear.

Men talk of killing time, while time quietly kills them.

Dion Boucicault (1820-90)

If gardening is a way of 'killing time',
we clearly need another thing to do.
But what? The problem with retiring now
is often 'killing time' and time that's new.

'Killing time' and 'filling time' are different –
we ought to work out which we're doing, fast.
And if we're simply killing time when gardening,
we might conjecture just how long we'll last.

You know you're a hard-core gardener when you deadhead in other people's gardens.

Sue Careless

Would I? Well, I might be tempted,
but think I'd leave dead heads alone,
unless the owner wasn't watching
and I was out there on my own.
Does that make me the hard core type?
I think I'm more a soft core sort,
who might deadhead if left unseen
but not if likely to be caught!

Snowy, flowy, blowsy,
showery, flowery, bowery,
hoppy, choppy, droppy,
breezy, sneezy, freezy.

'The Twelve Months' by George Ellis (1753-1815)

Same weather all year?
How dull that would be!
No difference at all?
No, that's not for me.
How dull in gardens
if nothing much changed.
No change in weather
would make me deranged.

The art of pleasing consists in being pleased.

The Round Table *by William Hazlitt (1778-1830)*

Cross with what the garden's doing?
Annoyed with it? Too much to do?
Gosh, are we pleasing friends far less?
I dearly hope that isn't true!
Are we grumpier in winter,
now fed up with our outside spot?
Oh dear, I fear that may be true,
while hoping strongly that it's not!

Total grief is like a minefield, no knowing when one will touch the tripwire.

Sylvia Townsend Warner (1893-1978)

Total grief – yes, like a minefield
with no clear path to go ahead,
but going outside – that can help
when in a state of grief or dread.

Less tripwires out there, many less,
and comforts in the silences
reflecting on what you have lost.
A kindly place your garden is.

Instead of tripping over wires
you're in a safer place to be –
a gentle, calming, soothing space
and road to your recovery.

Total grief is like a minefield.
I know – it's quite beyond belief.
But gardens help – and *how* they do
when plunged in all-consuming grief.

A poisoned chalice

When giving birds a drink in wintertime,
we may well think that we are being nice,
but if we put out water that is warm
we may not know some birds will pay the price.

People kindly putting out warm water,
(while thinking that it will not freeze as fast)
do not realise, for several birds there,
that day may sadly spell their very last.

They love the water; gorgeous, soothing, warm –
oh, such a comfort when it's freezing cold!
But not for long, not for long, so sadly,
and lots of them won't grow an hour more old.

The problem is, they go and bathe in it
and then the poor things often freeze to death.
Half an hour after that nice shower,
they may well gasp and take a final breath.

I wish that I'd been told that as a child.
Unwitting killer, that was sadly me.
I can but hope these words save feathered friends
and help avert more needless tragedy.

After every December follows always a May.

Wartime song in Germany, Lale Anderson (1905-72)

Cheer up all you gardeners! Forget the heating bill!
Forget the ghastly weather and too much time to kill!
After each December, there always comes a May.
Smile! Stay optimistic! It's not that far away!

A teacher affects eternity. He can never tell where his influence stops.

The Education of Henry Adams *by Henry Brooks Adams (1838-1918)*

Welcome to my winter art class.
I've chosen plants to paint this week.
And *please* don't look so disappointed.
Not all their hues are dull and bleak!

Think of jolly holly berries
and gorgeous yellow wintersweet,
and pink or scarlet cyclamens
or winter cherries – hard to beat!

So often winter students think
that flowers won't be fun to paint,
but wait and see the ones I've brought
with colours anything but faint.

Such a common misconception
thinking winter plants are duller.
Not true. In fact, a lot of them
give us even *stronger* colour.'

The frost performs his secret ministry, unhelped by any wind.

Samuel Taylor Coleridge (1772-1834)

The frost performs its secret ministry,
and to us gardeners, what a misery!
Too many plants we haven't taken in –
now sadly destined for the compost bin.
An early frost, unhelped by any wind,
means far too many, every year, are binned.

Will you love me in December as you do in May?

James J. Walker (1881-1946)

Not if it's the garden asking.
I'd have to say, 'No way!'
I can't love you in December
as once I did in May.

Not if it's the garden asking.
No, I don't love the cold.
No, I can't love you half as much,
not when the year is old!

A total frost descended

Jack Frost – once a marvellous artist
whose work we'll never see again.
Remember all those ferns and plants
he painted on each window pane?

Do you remember Jack, like me,
and all the plants he used to draw?
All gone now with central heating.
It's sad his work is seen no more.

No abstracts – always swirling plants,
and mostly ferns – miraculous.
The curls and swirls left on the panes
were always such a thrill for us.

Each window like a forest path
with plants I'd never seen before,
or ones I'd seen, but lovelier,
but never will see any more.

Our bedroom was a gallery –
a row of windows with his art.
However freezing cold we were,
his artwork always warmed the heart.

Waking up in freezing bedrooms
was not much fun when I was small.
Then, when looking at the windows,
we didn't mind the cold at all.

An artist not missed nowadays,
at least by anyone who's young.
But what a shame his artistry
is long forgotten and unsung.

Long melted into history books,
though not a book I've ever read.
But Jack, I still remember you,
in winter, getting out of bed.

Sock it to me!

Goldie Hawn

A bulb or two. A card for Kew.
A hand fork, seeds for something new.
Gardeners, always very easy
to give a Christmas present to!

Secateurs, a garden diary,
perhaps a planting DVD.
Gardeners, always very easy –
people just like you and me!

A penknife, gardening calendar.
Planting tabs are also nice.
You know the little things we like,
and won't fork out too high a price.

Sock it to us, anything,
seeds and things that we can use.
If it does some good out there,
everything is brilliant news!

The lack of money is the root of all evil.

Mark Twain (1835-1910)

It's now December, time for looking back,
remembering the money spent on plants.
Now, how to get our finances on track?
With Christmas round the corner, little chance!
Gardens all eat money if we let them,
and letting them we very often do.
Alas, it's sometimes better to forget them
and long before each Christmas time is due.
One week to Christmas – that can be a nightmare,
with loads of presents that we haven't bought.
We gave too many presents to the garden,
and now the cash is running pretty short.
Best to stop all planting in the summer
or even better, by the end of spring,
or Christmas can become a total nightmare;
the time a gardener can't afford a thing!

Tempus fugit

Virgil (70-19 BC)

Every year flies faster than the last one,
and every single winter comes too soon.
Where's the sun? It's getting ever weaker,
and disappearing by mid-afternoon.
Every year flies faster than the last one.
Is that a sign that we are getting old?
Or just a common moan of many gardeners
who don't much like their gardens when it's cold?

Most people ignore most poetry because most poetry ignores most people.

Adrian Mitchell (1932-2008)

My goodness, I agree with you!
I'm hoping that's what I *don't* do.
By picturing the reader, though,
and several gardeners whom I know,
I truly hope I don't ignore
the people whom I'm writing for.

Poems written for the poet –
now commonplace, and don't we know it!
But all this book attempts to do
is plant a happy smile or two
and dig into a gardener's soul.
Here's hoping I achieve that goal.

So much verse, self-regarding stuff.
By no means all, but quite enough,
especially in this day and age
that stop us reading in mid-page,
and snap the book shut there and then
and never glance at it again.

But if you like constructed rhymes
with rhythms used in former times
that do not look too inwardly,
you may enjoy this poetry.
I can but hope that's what I've done,
and gardeners find these poems fun!

And so to bed.

Samuel Pepys (1633-1703)

It's time, I think, to put this book to bed –
but all the work outside I simply dread.
So much outside in need of TLC
with too much time spent penning poetry!